ORIGINAL AUTHOR
NNETH GRAHAME
ADAPTED BY
CLAIRE O'BRIEN
ILLUSTRATED BY
DANIEL DUNCAN

The WIND in the WILLOWS

Contents

Chapter 1: The river bank

Rat and Mole stopped for a picnic.
There goes Toad in *another* brand new boat.
He'll soon get bored and buy something else.
Ha, ha! I'm such a clever Toad!

That's Badger. He doesn't come out much.
Maybe we could visit *him*?
No, he'll come to us when he's ready.

Mole tried rowing.
Careful!
Oh dear!

I can't swim!
Don't worry, Mole, I'll get you!
Rat dragged Mole to safety and took him home to dry off.
SPLOOSH! SPLASH!

Would you like to stay with me for a while? I'll teach you how to row and swim.
Oh, yes please.

One sunny day, Rat and Mole decided to visit Toad.
Hooray! Welcome to the finest house on the river!
Oh my!
Come and see my lovely new caravan!
We'll set off this afternoon!
What? No! We're not coming!
I can't possibly manage without you.
It does look fun …

This is the way to travel! The whole world is open to us …
I miss the river.
Hang on, what's that?

HUMMM!
BRUMMM!

POOP!
POOP!
POOP!

Steady boy!

Villains! Highwaymen! Scoundrels!

That's the way to travel!
POOP! POOP! POOP!

Several weeks later, Badger paid a visit. He brought serious news.
Toad has wrecked seven new motor cars!
Seven?!
And now he's bought *another* one.
We must try to teach him to be sensible.
We're going to have a serious talk.
Please take the car back to the shop.
You have wasted lots of money, Toad.
I'm so sorry, Badger.

You are giving animals a bad name.
I'm really very sorry, Badger.
Talking to him won't make any difference.

You are a dangerous driver, Toad.
I will give up motor cars forever.
SNIFF! BLUBBER! SOB!
Toad sounds very upset.

Toad is cured.
That's very good news!
Hmmm …

I'm *not* sorry at all.

I'm free! What a clever, handsome Toad I am.

A car! … It won't hurt to just *look* at it.
But a few moments later …
Stop, thief!
I am Toad, the Terror of the Road!
POOP!
POOP!
POOP!

It wasn't long before Toad was caught.
He was in serious trouble.
Twelve months for theft.
Three years for furious driving.
Fifteen years for being cheeky,
and one extra. Twenty years!
WAIL!
SOB!
HOWL!

Chapter 2: Toad's escape

Later that evening …
Jailer, let me out! I'm just the washerwoman, collecting washing.

I didn't see you come in.
You must've been having a nap.

Toad was very afraid of being caught.

But he was eventually out in the fresh air.

I'm free!

Toad was soon being chased.
Stop! Stop!
CHUFFA!
CHUFFA!
CHUFFA!
Policemen!
The train went through a tunnel.
There's only one thing for it!

wHEEEEE!
wHoOOOO!

Ha, ha!
I'm such a clever
Toad!

However, it wasn't long before Toad
was cold, hungry and very tired.

He had to sleep under some leaves.
No proper bed.
Nothing for supper.
No money.

Oh miserable
Toad!

In the morning, Toad found the road, but he had a nasty surprise.
Oh no! That's the car I stole! What if I'm captured? Chains again! Prison again! Dry bread and water again!

Oh unhappy Toad! Oh despair!

However, Toad was lucky.
This poor old washerwoman has fainted.
Let's take her to the village.
Hooray!

How do you feel now, madam?
I'd feel much better if I could sit in the front.
Of course!

Could I have a go at driving?
Why not? It won't do any harm.

Toad went faster …

… and faster … and faster still … until …
Be careful!
Slow down, washerwoman!

Washerwoman indeed! I'm fearless Toad!
You stole our car!
Seize him!

I'm a Toad-bird!

Soon, Toad was on the run again.
Uh oh!

He leapt into a river to escape.
SPLASH!

Toad was carried down the river.
He saw a familiar face.
Oh Ratty!

Back at Rat's house …
I've had some terrible times, Rat.
Yes, all because you were stupid and stole a motor car!

I'll go straight back to Toad Hall and be sensible.

You mean you haven't heard?
Heard what?
About the stoats and weasels?

They said you were never coming back. They've taken over Toad Hall.
The Wild Wooders? At Toad Hall?
SNIFF! SNIFF!

Mole and Badger stuck up for you. They stayed at Toad Hall and looked after it.

But hundreds of weasels and stoats attacked them with sticks and threw them out.
This is our place now!
You'll be sorry!
They've made a terrible mess and said that they intend to stay for good.
What? We'll soon see about that!

Get out of my house at once or I'll …
Or you'll what …?

SPLAT!

TWANG!

Outrageous! How dare they!
SPLAT!
SPLOT!
OUCH!

I promise to listen to your advice in future.
HOWL!
WAIL!
SOB!
In that case we will have supper, go to bed and wait for Mole and Badger.

Chapter 3: Taking back Toad Hall

Why didn't my father tell me about it?
Because you can't keep a secret.
Well, I suppose I do like to chat a little bit.

The passage leads to the pantry.
Tonight is the Chief Weasel's birthday party.
Perfect! They will all be together.

We'll creep up on them.
And we'll chase them out!
We must prepare!
It will be a complete surprise.

The friends prepared for battle.
Flask … sandwich box … sticking-plasters … lantern.
ZZZZZ! ZZZZZ!
This won't take long.
Mole had an idea …

Got any washing today?
No! We never wash.
Run away, washerwoman!

It'll be you who's running away soon.
What d'you mean?

I've heard that a hundred bloodthirsty badgers are coming here tonight …
What?

… six boatloads of ruthless rats …

… a mob of murderous moles …

… and a gang of terrifying toads!

The weasels didn't tell us!
Typical weasels. They don't care about us stoats.
CHUCKLE CHUCKLE

Mole told the others.
Oh Moley! You didn't!
You silly creature! You've spoilt everything!

Clever Mole!
If they're expecting hundreds of us they'll be scared and run as soon as we attack.
Genius!

Why didn't I think of that?

After dark …
Ha, ha, ha!
URP!
HIC!
POP!
Hey! You've got more lemonade than me.
So what!

Meanwhile …
It's so dark and damp!
Come *on*, Toad!
No chattering or complaining, Toad, or you'll be sent back!

This is it. We're right under the pantry. Get ready all of you!
Happy birthday to you! Happy birthday to you …
Ready!
Yes, I'm ready.
Let me get hold of that Chief Weasel!
Follow me!
Badger threw the trap door open.
CHARGE!
Whack em!
HONK!
HONK!
Grrrrr!
RUN FOR IT!
AAARRGH!
EEK!

The weasels panicked.
It's the ruthless rats! Help!
It's the murderous moles! Let me out!
It's the terrible toads! We're finished!
SPLATTER!
CRASH!
SMASH!
SHOVE!

Some ran out of the doors …
You'd better move fast!
I'm going! I'm going!

… some fled up the chimney and got stuck …
Ha!

… and some went out of the windows.
Out you go!
Eek!

Toad chased the Chief Weasel.
I'll get you!
Let me through, I need a boat!

It was all over very quickly.
They've all gone!
Excellent! The battle is won!
You two can tidy up the bedrooms.
I think it's time for supper.

The weasels were very sorry.
We've left clean towels …
… and fresh sheets …
After a good supper, the friends made their way to bed feeling full of joy and contentment.
Thank you, Mole, for your plan. I see how clever you are now.
You showed great courage, Toad.

The next morning, after a good rest …
How wonderful to be back home.
You should hold a banquet to celebrate, Toad.
You can write the invitations this morning.
Certainly not! I want to enjoy myself today!
You *must* have a banquet. We'll order the food. Now go and write the invitations.
Toad suddenly changed his mind.
You're right, of course, Badger. I will write them.
He's up to something.

Toad had an idea.
This is an opportunity to tell everyone about my adventures and my bravery.
scribble, scribble
I'm such a clever Toad!
But Rat, Badger and Mole saw what he had written …
Toad's Banquet
Programme for the evening:
Speech - by Toad
Other speeches - by Toad
A song - by Toad
Further songs - by Toad
Mr Toad

No, Toad! There will be no speeches.
GASP!
And no songs!
It's for your own good.

Your speeches and songs are just showing off.
Just one *little* song.
No!
Toad became thoughtful. He knew that they were right.

At the banquet, he praised the others and was modest and quiet. It felt good.
Badger was the leader.
Rat and Mole did most of the fighting.
He was, indeed, a changed Toad.
Toad had become a much happier creature, and his friendship with Rat, Mole and Badger continued for many long summers.

Kenneth Grahame was born on 8th March 1859. He grew up in Scotland with his mother, father, sister and two brothers.

When he was five, his mother died of a nasty fever. Kenneth also caught the same illness but eventually recovered.

After that, Kenneth went to live in Berkshire with his grandmother. His new home was near the River Thames where he developed a lifelong passion for the river and for boating; it was no doubt an inspiration for *The Wind in the Willows.*

Kenneth went to school in Oxford and went on to work for the Bank of England. He married in 1899 and had one son, Alastair.

The Wind in the Willows was first published in 1908. The then President of the United States, Theodore Roosevelt, was a fan of the book. *The Wind in the Willows* has sold millions of copies and continues to be popular today.

Kenneth died at his home in Pangbourne, Berkshire on 6th July 1932.